**ANCHOR BOOKS**

MIRRORS OF THE MIND

Edited by

Steve Twelvetree

First published in Great Britain in 2000 by
ANCHOR BOOKS
Remus House,
Coltsfoot Drive,
Woodston,
Peterborough, PE2 9JX
Telephone (01733) 898102

All Rights Reserved

Copyright Contributors 2000

HB ISBN 1 85930 840 6
SB ISBN 1 85930 845 7

FOREWORD

Mirrors Of The Mind is a special anthology that contains the collective thought of over 160 poets.

New and established writers combine their talents to bring you an anothology that is fresh and uplifting whilst being a truly inspiring and ejoyable read.

With such a wide variety of views from an even wider range of people, this anthology is a must for anyone in need of poetic inspirations.

Steve Twelvetree
Editor

CONTENTS

ELEMENTS OF ENGLISH

By the light of an
Anglepoise
joy-riding *commas*
widely missed
their conjunction;
crashing into the
dimly lit margins.
There, unpleasant *verbs*
were doing-over
some nice *italics.*
Along the fine lines
above a famous quote;
Asterisk night dreamed
of being a heavenly
star.
Long lost *brackets*
hugged and reminisced
over years of being apart.
Exclamation mark
kept a polite distance
from the *expletives;*
standing close to
nervous *question mark*
who constantly
begged a question;
how else could it exist?

Josie May Hodges

BEAUTY

Nature is so wonderful
With all the joys it brings,
The trees, the flowers, the animals,
A summer bird that sings.
A graceful swan upon a lake,
A colourful butterfly,
All these and many more we see
As we go wandering by.
The early morning, moist with dew,
A web so fine with mist
And then the flowers opening
Are by the sunlight kissed.
Then the evening sunset
To herald end of day,
Another beauty to behold
As we go on our way.
We thank Thee, O Great Spirit,
For all these gifts we have
We know that you have given them
With all your boundless love.

Ruth Smith

CHANGING COLOURS OF AUTUMN

Autumn is the artist's dream
The golden hues of light
The fading of the evergreen
The golden glow by night

The cleverly crocheted webs are hung
On artists' frames by day
Turn crystal with the rising sun
When dry they fade away

The misty mysterious merging of the morn
When rabbits frolic and deers browse
Ever watchful, ever alert
Till the breaking of the dawn.

The fruits are now in plenty
The acorn and the berries
The king of nuts, the conkers ripe
And the crimson of the cherries

Burnished bronze of bracken
That rustle in the wind
Give view to stubbled fields of wheat
That once were bleached and tinged

The cold breath of winter
Stills the life within the trees
Whilst the leaves are snatched and
Whisked away by the ever blowing breeze

Caroline Purser

SANTA

Gliding through the air he goes,
Oh what's that with a big red nose?
It's Rudolph, Santa's favourite deer,
That's the one who has to steer.

He steers here to there from left to right
Gliding through the breezy night.
With presents for me and you,
With presents he's made all year through.

Just think when you're tucked up in bed at night
He comes in then, he's out of sight.
All the presents go under the tree,
To know what they are
You will have to wait and see!

Now it's morning, here comes the fun
All because what Santa's done!

Jade Hughes (13)

THE STRANGER

I saw a stranger raise his eyes
Above this world to sunlit skies
He gazed around for what he knew
Was in this wonderland of blue.
For here no sound disturbs the air
No unhappiness or care
Could ever find a resting place
Could ever crease the stranger's face.
This was a man who knew the world
And one whom cruel fate had hurled
Into the melting pot of life
To fight a long and bitter fight.
Yet even he forgets such things
For a little while his heart has wings
And understands serenity
And contemplates eternity.

R G Stevens

MUM'S PHOTOGRAPH
11TH FEBRUARY 1935

My eyes water meeting yours,
so tingling I become you draped by the flare of your
long curtain dress, with elbow length bell sleeves,
red square line velvet on shoulders.
Do I look alright? Gosh my skin feels hot.
This dress weighs a ton.
Tuck hair behind ears. Have the waves dropped? Look!
Pearl earrings, borrowed, the necklace is not.
Lipstick is daredevil red. What!
Matches my blush. Mischievousness. Smile!
In goose pimple nervousness?
They're playing Liberty Belle my tune and
I'm breathless, eighteen, all eager hopefulness,
poised to swing into my first dance,
filled with vital excitement of unknown years ahead.
Who brought you Mother six others before me.
Business kept you too busy but we are in your heart.
Now for the girl in thirties red -
life's a party with new friends,
Holidays. Rest? No bingo.
We love one another although we
don't understand each other.
We cry together.
Your smile chases my rain away.
We laugh together.
Mother, I knew what you meant when
one Tia Maria too many, you looked at me standing by
and said, 'Look after yourself.'

Mary Percival

INSPIRATION

You've given me a will to believe
That my fairy tale shall exist,
It's confirmed each time you hold me
And strengthened with every kiss.
My body is just a medium to provide a stage on which to play,
To act out my gestures of affection
To mimic the words my heart needs to say.
I give to you my heart to hold in place of our future's prosperity.
My soul you already own and bought with our past sincerity.
You captivate my warmth; you induce a harmful desire,
You see past my insecurities and you never fail to inspire.
I pay homage to our love
For the touch that brings affection.
For the days that have brought me your smile
And your arms that have offered protection.
You compliment my nature with the seeds of change you've planted,
You've rendered me incapable with the feeling of bliss I'm granted.
I give to you all that I am and all I aspire to be,
I owe you much more in return for all you have given me.

Hayley Beddoes

Moon Through Fog

Faint corpuscle, dripping tap
Wearing a bridal smoke.
Stubbed out sun, wing mirror
Thin papyrus of a bottom drawer.

Some reedy corncrake, last harvest,
Undone button, graffiti full stop.
Circle of static, silent semibreve
Humming to a Quaker chimney.

Tenish orphan phantom
Face of a gas mask
Ticked off nought
Misty lycanthrope.

Your teeth have been muzzled,
Smog and mesh, tides are still.
Grey spooned sockets glare
Blinded eyes, Earthly pale.

A J Strange

THE VALLEY OF DREAMS

A silhouette in the eventide
Stands the little grey house alone
And bats come flitting in and out
Of the ruins and mossy stone.

Honeysuckle hangs in the doorway,
The quaint old broken-down arch,
And the moon rises over the hilltops
That are crowned with fir tree and larch.

Now scented spikes of lavender
And the fragrance of stock and rose
Fill the air with dreamy softness
And the longing for repose.

I lie on the tree-sheltered hillock
On the brink of the waters of peace.
No more shall I wake in the morning,
For the evening will never cease.

I am lost in the still sleep of ages
By the side of the rest-giving streams.
No tumult will ever disturb me,
For this is the Valley of Dreams.

Kay Gilbert

TAKEN FOR A RIDE

A metallic monster with a powerful heart
    driven with expertise,
purring engine slowly dies,
    eerie silence.

Trepidation enters a confused mind,
sudden delusion as ultimatum is stipulated,
    cannot win either way,
briny tears flood fearful eyes.

Pleads earnestly against unwanted advances,
revulsion as strength and dominance takes over,
    cries of panic cut no ice
depraved action concluded, contempt rains down.

Tortured soul, mind and body
cast aside into oblivion,
metallic monster with a powerful heart
    driven by a maniac
engine roaring, vanishes into the night.

Gill Whyman

On Kath And Ralph's Wedding Anniversary

To Kath and Ralph let me express
Congrats on years of happiness
As hand-in-hand you go through life
Without a care or any strife.

The memories of the years gone by
Will no doubt make you wonder why
You look so young and full of vigour
And Kath still keeps her sylph-like figure.

Many congratulations to you both.

T N Fisher

FAREWELL KISS

Once I saw the
Man in the moon
From my bedroom
A shooting star
Seemed
Very Far
That's why
As dawn crept
My mother wept
Her farewell kiss
Upon
My pillow.

Andréa Selina Bennett

THE FLOWER

There's a dead flower in the vase,
Standing withered and left alone,
I should discard it, throw it away,
But then there's no reminder
Of the beautiful bouquet.

So bright, so fresh and vibrant,
The scent, then exquisite has now gone,
Why do I cling to this dead flower
For it can't revive - regenerate
Even given a healing summer shower?

What a waste! All that beauty gone,
Was the pleasure worth the pain?
For those sweet flowers will never, never
Never, bloom again.
And they were allowed no precious time to seed,
Plucked in haste, by men of greed -
To further their own ends.

Stevie-Jo

THAT'S ENTERTAINMENT

Thespians snore, sneeze, belch
and stammer,
As per inclusions in the
author's grammar,
Yet none breaks wind in a
costume drama,
Such life-like graphicness is
not today sought . . .

Or is it . . . ?

Perhaps in, (as yet unknown),
physiological ways,
Folk simply didn't do it
in those days,
Or, in a manner we've failed
to suss,
It was done, but differently
from us.

Now . . . there's a thought.

Frank Valentine

FLOODS OF AFRICA

A life's work has been washed away
By the greatest floods.
People are left homeless and cold.
Their families have been torn apart.
Children have been left orphans.
Everything gone in a second,
Homes, animals, people all washed away.
Where there once was land and trees,
There's only muddy water and death.
All this has happened to these poor people
Who need help from you and I.
When I first saw it on TV
It made me feel sad and cry.
How lucky we are not to live there,
So we must do what we can
To help build their lives back together
In their time of great need
In this terrible disaster.

Autum Taylor

WENDY'S BEREAVEMENT (1999)
(From Liz with love)

Your father has gone,
Your mum has too,
And now in retrospect,
Perhaps you have a regret . . .
Childhood memories,
Togetherness and stories,
Bereavement tears,
For all the lost years.
The future seems bleak,
As a tear falls on your cheek,
But wait a while,
Because again you will smile.
In illness you were there,
Although at times difficult to bear,
Unnecessary to say,
You were there day to day.
He heard your voice,
In your presence he did rejoice,
Despite his inability,
And lack of capability . . .
Now think a while,
Accept his thanks and smile,
'Reunion', with his wife,
Has given him a new life . . .

Liz Edwards

DEUS EX MACHINA

Freedom screams from the backstreets,
It's hungry and it's worn;
It's maxed out on credit,
And it's ready to soar.
Wallowing in acid,
Full of rips and burns,
It struggles in the smoke:
Time to end this charade.
Freedom lies in a blue and green holdall.
Freedom lies wrapped in a pink coverall.
Freedom is hacked up into pieces and left
      by the roadside to decompose.
She ties her hair in red ribbon,
Robs banks and exploits the weak.
Her insides are full of flies,
As she rots and is abused again.
Bought and sold with a wicked currency,
Dissolved in a rancid apathy,
Hold her up honey and garrotte her with
      your fine gold wire -
And make her choke as you feed her your
        fine bone china,
Then display her corpse for all your friends to see.
Hung in the air and grasped by deceit.
Is it you that has sinned
Or our saviour, our saint?

Danielle Green

IT'S TRUE! I LOVE YOU!

It's true! I love you!
How can I prove to you that it is true?
I do! I love you!
There must be some way I can show it's true!
I'd climb a mountain,
Or face an angry tiger in its lair!
Cross the burning desert!
Stand excruciating pain!
If it proves to you how much I care!

I do! I love you!
If only I could prove to you it's true!
It's true! I love you!
I'll show it's true in everything I do!
Not just with kisses
Or making love, the way I do with you,
Everything I do
Will be to make you tell me 'yes',
You believe me when I say, 'It's true!'

Geoff O'Neil

MYTH OR FACT

The Danes they came from a far off land,
With dogs of terror to make their mark,
Rumour spread throughout the land of large black dogs roaming wild.
Folk law tells the tales today of people's fright when out at night.

The hound of Odin,
Mighty dog of war,
Stalking highways all night long,
Black Shuck became its name,
Warning of impending death.
Seen in many countries throughout the land spreading fear near and far.

Many villages of today, remember dogs of yesterday,
Bringing to mind one on a sea front known for good deeds,
And another charging through the local church,
Killing all in sight.

The Danes aim was achieved for superstition was ripe at night.

G F Snook

SNOW IN THE NIGHT

How white is snow?
Is it as white
        as the heat of a kiln that fires a pot in the night?
No, not that bright.
Is it as white as the flashing teeth of a star
        or the pearls that she wears in the evening light?
No, not that white.

How cold is snow?
Is it as cold
As youth that is brash and bold?
No, not so cold.
Is it as cold as the frost that freezes our bones
                as we grow old?
No, not so cold.

How pure is snow?
Is it as pure
As the wings of the swan on the mere?
Is it as pure as the sweet white rose, the lilac,
        the blossom that drifts to my door?
No, not so pure.

How soft is snow?
Is it as soft
As ermine in grandmother's muff, as soft as newly hatched
        ducklings' fluff, as soft as a cloud aloft?
No, not so soft.

How still is snow?
Is it as still as a baby's wonder, a baby's breath,
As still as love, as still as death? . . .
No, not so still.

How bright is snow?
When it falls in the night, obscuring all stars,
Shimmering with its own light, to glimmer
                                and bring to our sight
A softened and glistening landscape,
                        sleeping around us, aglow, alight,
Fashioned of six-pointed crystals refracting the light,
Yes, so bright, so still,
                    so soft, so pure,
                            so cold, so white,
                                    is the snow in the night.

Sylvia Tyers

The Seeds

If we could sow the seeds of love
　　Like we sow our wheat and corn
Just to sow those seeds of love
　　To start a great new dawn
There are so many beautiful things to see
　　From our gods these gifts are free
No matter what form He may take
　　He still loves you and me
So let's start thinking of our loved ones
　　Let the world stop thinking of the gun
If each and everyone of us
　　Would sow these precious seeds
To give them all away with love
　　And pray to God above
Then all our little children
　　Could share a paradise

Alf

A Road To Nowhere

I've got this far, but where to now?
    The track's come to an end.
A battered signpost gives no help,
    Its letters can't be read.
There isn't anyone to ask,
    I'm thirsty, hungry, tired,
I'd hoped to reach a village soon,
    Or even find a barn.
Ah well, it's no good giving up
    I'd better just plod on!

Joy Wyhowska

THE CHANGING SEASONS

See on the dark, bare trees
A mist of palest green,
The herald of the spring,
Cold winter in retreat.

Each tree brings forth its leaves
In all their varying shades,
The silver birch so fair,
The copper beech green-bronze.

And there upon the boughs
The catkin and the flower,
Red, yellow, pink and white
Among the fluttering leaves.

And autumn brings a change
To russet, brown and red
And every shade between
As winter closes in.

Once more the boughs are black
Against the darkening sky.
The once green leaves now lie
Upon the sleeping earth.

Heather Brackley

LOVE'S NOT JUST

Love stubbornly invades
Our private world
Aspects of emotions
Stirred a whirl

Ecstatically happy
Depressively sad
Turmoil of feelings
Wonders to be had

Savouring moments
Of love's play
Carefree happy
Heartstrings astray

Unexpected rejection
Looms its ugly head
Emotional senses
Realism ahead

Heartache betrayal
Of innocent trust
Pride hiding tears
Love's not just.

Isabelle Wright

REMEMBRANCE DAY

There it stood, almost dejected, its fiery red petals blazing against the
insipid colours of grey which covered the concrete ribbon of the
motorway.

What was it doing there? Why had it chosen to grow so aloof, out of its
natural surroundings?
In an alien place; yet commanding so much beauty, which time
eventually would erase!
As I ponder on these thoughts, I remembered the symbol of the poppy
related to times of war and bloodshed;
Of the greyness and the futility of war and how so many brave, young
lives were also placed in alien surroundings.
I thought of how their blood was shed and covered the dark, grey
muddy soil and, of their glorious sacrifice and suffering
for the sake of their country;
I felt sorrow for their mothers, who waited anxiously for news, and
grieved continually for their precious, lost sons!

My mind and spirit darkened as I slowly reminisced, though I
gradually realised that,
Just as the poppy on that motorway seemed to be a light shining
in the darkness,
Conversely, the symbol of the poppy, with its transient life,
reminded me that time would never erase the memories
of the pain and misery of war!
For we shall remember them on the eleventh hour, on the eleventh day,
of the eleventh month of every year,
To ensure that their blood was not shed in vain!
Rest in peace!

Rita A Kemp

ON ARRIVING AT HENGRAVE HALL

Late afternoon sun,
Water dark and deep, with ripples.
Snowdrops,
Last year's beechnut husks,
A church made of cobbles.
Quiet,
Intense, peaceful quiet.
Quiet you can lean on.
May peace prevail on Earth.
Stone floors,
Timber,
Vaulted ceilings,
Heavy wooden doors.
Pollarded trees,
Flints in the gravel.
The Sisters dressed in purple.
May peace prevail on Earth.
Grace at suppertime.
A small flint cottage,
Just one bedroom.
Quiet
Intense, peaceful quiet,
Quiet you can lean on.
May peace prevail on Earth.

Maureen Cahill

As Time Goes By

When I was young and in my prime
I got presents all the time.

In my twenties it would be
Chocolates, flowers and jewellery.

Then when I got my first home
It was saucepans and a garden gnome.

When older and with a family
My gifts were meant for them you see.

The forties and fifties were a sell,
I even got gifts for the car as well.

But in my sixties I wondered when
I would get presents for myself again.

And what did I get for myself at last?
A plastic case for my old bus pass.

Pauline Anderson

OUR PRAISES TO GOD . . .

We must give thanks, and sing praises,
Unto our Lord,
And to raise our heads,
And stand upright,
To show loving, kindness, and faith,
Throughout the day, and the night,
We must worship our Lord,
And kneel to Him, with rapture,
Because He is our only God,
And we are His pasture,
He looks down from heaven,
Through the clouds, and walks,
Upon the wings of the wind,
To guide us to our work, and play,
And then comes the evening,
When we can all thank Him,
For His everlasting love,
When we kneel to Him, and pray . . .

John A Shaw

MY BLUE HEAVEN

When winter winds blow chill
And snow lies deep down the lane
I sit by my fireside and dream
And I'm back in the springtime again.
And my dream will always take me
To the place I love so well
Deep, deep into the forest
Of the scented sweet bluebell.
Mid those heavenly fragranced flowers
That reflect the bright blue sky
They blanket in profusion
Over fell and banks they lie.
Enchantment strange and heady
Surrounded this perfect place
Where only rabbits and squirrels
Disturb the peaceful pace.
A wondrous sight, from heaven sent
Were my thoughts when there I stood
For nowhere can compare in spring
To the beautiful bluebell wood.
So when in winter the bluebells rest
And snowflakes fall all around
I sit by my fireside reflecting
On the times they embellished the ground.
With the warmth of the flames
For my sunshine
I am back with the bluebells there
Back in that perfumed forest
Far away from the wintry white air.

Constance I Roper

MY MAN

He told me how he liked the look of Linda's
                                    golden curls
He said that he admired Jane's skirt, especially
                                    when she whirls
He wondered where on earth Miranda got that
                                    stunning hat
The green one with the fluffs and frills, just
                                    like the bathroom mat
Yet when he caught me unawares, my aching
                                    eyes half-closed
Different from the other girls, with no lovely
                                    golden curls
That's when he proposed

Christine Lacey

MEMORIES OF RAIN

Soggy socks on the bathroom floor,
Waterlogged shoes.
Rain drenched umbrella dripping,
Smell of damp.
Droplets snaking down the window pane,
Gutters gurgling,
Drains brimming full.
Puddles inviting feet,
to jump and splash.

Nicola Grant

FOR CHILDREN

Two thousand years ago
In a town called Bethlehem
A family tired and cold
Were told,
No room at the inn,
So that child was born
In a stable,
He came to purge the world of sin.

Come forward two thousand years
A dome was built to celebrate
The second millennium,
There is no room within that dome,
To celebrate that birth in Bethlehem.

While politicians offer each other praise,
Call it their millennium prayer.
Across the darkened river's chill
Through the freezing air,
Across two thousand years
Echoes the cry of a child
Lonely, hungry, cold,
For whom there is still
No room at the inn.

No room at the Millennium Dome
For the story of Bethlehem.

Arthur J Pullen

THREE SCORE YEARS AND TEN

At ten I went to grammar school,
I didn't like it much.

At twenty when the army called
I did my bit as such.

At thirty I got married,
Had a family of two.

At forty suffered depression,
In hospital I did go.

At fifty I left for a group home
So dear.

At sixty I left for a bedsit
Near.

I often wonder what seventy will bring,
Oh well, 'Che sera' I sing.

Doreen Bacon

LONDON AIR RAIDS

I remember
the hard steel meshed bunks
on platforms
where the tube train stopped.
Then rushed on into the tunnel.

I remember
disjointed sleep beside my mother
in the dim light
as people walked up and down,
going nowhere.
Waiting
for the all clear.

I remember
the necessary, disinfectant filled buckets
behind sackcloth curtains.
Dreaded.

I remember asking why.

Susanne Shalders

MARRIED LIFE

Together at last, two hearts beat as one
Now your married life has begun.
No one knows what will come your way,
Communication, let each have their say!
Give and take but mostly give,
Treat each other, as you'd like to live.
Understanding, plays a very large part,
Let one another know what's in your heart.
And when you feel you're at the end
Remember your partner is also your friend!
Sometimes you know, you come very close
To hating the one you love the most!
But the hard times - they won't last forever,
Remember the love that drew you both together.
Respect is something that you must earn,
So take time to listen, take time to learn.
Whatever you do affects the other one's life
Now you've decided to be *man* and *wife!*
Cherish the moment, be always true
To yourself . . . and your other half too!

Christine Peers

NEW BEGINNING

It's like the first ray of sun at daybreak,
The sweet fresh smell after the rain has fell,
The sharpness of a frost,
The strength of the wind,
The birds sweetly singing their chorus of the morning,
All these remind me of a new start,
A new beginning.

Emma Matthews

IF ONLY I HAD WINGS

I wish I had wings like a bird and could fly in the sky,
I know if I had the chance I would really try.
I would sit high upon the chimneys and look around
And watch all the people working on the ground.
I would sit on the telephone wire to have a swing
And watch out for the cat when his bell starts to ring.
I would love a little mate to help me build a nest,
Then we could have little babies and be like all the rest.
I have found some bread on the lawn for me to sit and eat,
Then I will go in the bird bath to wash my wings and feet.
I am going with my little friends to fly away tonight,
So look out for us tomorrow we will be somewhere in your sight.

Colin H Cross

CITY LIVING

I went into town today,
What an experience, one must say.
There was a man playing his flute,
A puppet dancing, worked by his foot!

People were swarming everywhere.
The crowds I left behind me there.
Down by the river I did ride,
'Twas quiet, and like the countryside.

I called in to see Graham on my way home.
My son did ask, 'Wherever did you roam?
You went for the newspaper.
I was wondering how long does it take her?

I thought you had met with another accident.
Its been two hours since you went.
You are looking well to me.
This is very pleasing to see!'

Barbara Joan Shaw

IT

How can I fight what I cannot see
Slowly, slowly tugging at me
Suction waiting until my back is turned
It's going to claw me, it cannot be heard
So how can I fight what I cannot see?

To contemplate a vision not seen
A feeling of dusk is ready to descend
It will deaden the light that comes from within

Midway through August I am taken away
Only to be replaced with torture and pain
Mind lame, a mutilated mess
I know this is not me at my best

It takes away my colour
I fade away
Exist in the outer shell
Holding on till I am rid of this hell

Jane Patricia Collie

THE WINTER SLEEP

Winter has come, no more sun
All the fields look so bleak
The cold upon us did creep
Brown earth is resting
The grass lies dormant
No need to mow
Seed wait for me to sow
When the spring comes
Again we'll see the sun
New plants will grow
Crops again we will own
Now the winter wind blows
On the ground frost glows
All the earth is asleep
Nothing for us to reap
A time for all to rest
Waiting for the spring to come
Then we all greet the sun

Kathleen Fry

MOMENTS

Moments are like rainbows,
They just happen,
from the birth of a child to falling in love again.

A moment of joy, that the camera
can snap,
And of victories, that come out of all
our mishaps!

To a sunny day, when all the world seems alright,
A moment of togetherness, when the future
looks bright.

That time, we saw the valleys, and
pleasant lands,
And when we held each other's hands

And when I was lonely, a friend did knock
on my door,
And moments of heartache, we all can endure.

And a moment that changed my views
that all these precious things,
Out of moments that come true.

The moment, I had to grab it fast,
That now, yesterday, our moments
have gone past.

As I look at the rainbow dissolve in the sky
I treasure these moments, till the day I die.

D Riches

ALF ALFINA

Alf is my little Persian kitten.
Alf is short for Alfina.
She is so beautiful, all silver grey and white.
Her eyes are large, amber in colour
with large black pupils.
She just has to look at you with those
bright amber eyes and she gets just what she wants.
She loves to sit and watch the fire burning bright.
Her favourite thing is a bath, then a brush and a talc,
That really makes her swagger.
With her tail in the air she gives a meow,
As if to say, 'No I'm not Alf, I'm Alfina.'
Then she settles down with a contented purr
until the fire goes out.

Judith Balchin

IN SCAWBY WOODS

A grey gull's nest lies in the wood
Where Devil's Bit and Filbeards hide
The twig has lost the warming breast
That moved the Hellebore beside
Her circled leaves and badger fur
And the dead bark that winters bring
Shelter to an ageing thin white web
That fluffs her empty wing.

A grey gull's shadow haunts the ground
Where ploughs turn top soil from the sun
And further to the glow of steel
They circle, black and white, but one
Half seeing, saw in the distant wood
Well sheltered and half full of leaves
Her nest caught in the damp of evening
That the mist finger weaves.

A grey gull's nest unwanted still
Over the bog and bracken flame
Where saffron threads of winter fill
Each loneliness, beneath the same
Broad sky of bush and tree
That bends each turret bough in vain
To urge, as celandine the sun,
A grey gull back again.

W E Hobson

The Seasons

Seasons come and seasons go,
God in heaven planned it so,
We welcome the coming of the spring
When all of nature is renewing
All the plants, the flowers, the trees
Awake once more from winter freeze
The daffodils they look so gay
Tossing their heads in bright array.
Then follows summer with warmer days,
When all the gardens are ablaze
With lovely colours of every hue
Giving us cheer the whole day through.
Autumn brings the harvest in,
Of corn and fruit, all mellowing.
The changing colours of the greenery
Adds to the beauty of the scenery.
The days are shorter when winter's here,
Cold and damp and dark and drear
With rain and sleet and frost and snow
We stay indoors with fires aglow.
Seasons come and seasons go,
All because God planned it so.

V Hankins

OUR RUTH

You were a sweet little girl
So pretty, all sugar and spice
But you were such a tomboy
Wore your brother's old T-shirts and jeans
Even though they were old and frayed at the seams
You copied everything he did
You followed him everywhere
He made you laugh a lot
He'd look around him
And you were always there.
You hated dressing tidy and neat
'I'm not wearing that' you would say
Hands on hips and stamping your feet.
Where have the years all gone?
Now you're our little girl no more
But I still see you there in your oversized jeans
Pigtails hanging down and ribbons in streams
And all of your life, I want you to know
Whatever you do and wherever you go
I'll always remember you
Ribbons hanging in streams
Standing there a small tomboy
In T-shirt and jeans.

Margaret Pay-Watson

A BONFIRE

Is there any greater pleasure
      Watching curling smoke at leisure
At dusk the pile is Everest
      Too high for safety in the gathering gloom.

Early dawn shows no sign,
      The pile is black as night.
No flickering flames to strike terror in the heart,
      But hot as hell itself inside.

Is there any greater pleasure
      Watching curling smoke at leisure
At dawn it rises through the mist
      And beckons with increasing measure.

My boots await, a warm coat, the air is still.
      Can one resist the call, to stir to life
The flickering flames and watch the smoke arise?

Is there any greater pleasure
      Watching curling smoke at leisure
Black as night the sky above
      The heavens open once again
To dampen down the flickering flames.

Eileen M Stupples

ODE TO BRIGG

Those old courts and alleys, the ginnels and entries
And terraced houses, with tunnels passing through them,
At front ends of which, wheelie bins stand like sentries,

       Call up Brigg, no error.

Years' worth of dust, caught in a shabby net curtain's hem
Hung against passage-facing windows, will stem
Pedestrians' espionage, in a second.
Without mistake; such northern aspects evoke Brigg.
From fifty or so miles, they have always beckoned me
And their appeal smoulders like a fizgig.

Gillian C Fisher

THE PICTURE

A picture hangs upon the wall
Of the house that I detest
It looks like a cow-shed
Or a garage at its best.
Auntie gave the picture
One day when she called
But really that picture
Is an eyesore to us all.
The walls are painted sickly green
The shape is nondescript.
When I showed my friends the picture
They very nearly flipped.
One day we had burglars
How I cried when I saw the mess
But finding they had taken the picture
My tears turned to happiness.

Jenny Bosworth

IN THE AIR

I'm a rhyme
Given time
I can wax a'lyrical
can be quite hysterical
something of a miracle
But I'm a rhyme
Given time!

You may listen
sit and stare
But something's coming
way out there
Where it comes from
I don't care
But I'm a rhyme
given time!

Interesting alliterations
Metaphors and
Connotations
exacting exciting exaggerations
Maybe some deliberations
But I'm a rhyme
Given time!

Just some rhythm
Mixed with rhyme
Metrical, electrical
Sparkling highly systemetrical
Where it comes from
I don't care
Just a rhyme from way out there!

Theresa A Eady

STALKER

Haunting breath of stalking stealth
stealing light 'neath glimmered moon
tracking treadfall, scattered leaf
whispered sweep of blustered broom
movement glimpsed, flickered eyes
invoking imagination's wrath to stir
trembled limbs, quaking spirit shell
soul stripped naked, fear laid bare
tangled hedgerow hiding silent shades
closing shadows, seeping, creeping chill
startled spectre, creature of the night
timid thudding heart beating still

Paul Birkitt

JILTED

Squeeze my heart
bleed it dry
swelling tears
free to cry
feel the hurt
feel the pain
standing silent
soaking rain
raging emotion
fires burn
nowhere to hide
nowhere to turn

Chris Bailey

ZOMBIE MUM!

I saw a film the other night, it was full of zombies, you know the kind.
Blood, guts and lots of gore, high pitched screams and not a trace
of story line.
I kept hiding my face, I could handle the ripped off limbs,
the puss filled pores and the menacing groans, I just couldn't stand
the fact that the creature before me looked just like me.
I was once a teenager looker, vain to a degree with long brown hair,
perky breasts and sparkling eyes.
I had a waist back then and firm smooth thighs.
I would wear the tightest skirts to show what I had,
I was once told that I oozed sex and my shy smile would melt
the coldest heart.
I would get excited about the silliest things and each new day was
awaited with anticipation.
The years have gone and so have the breasts, the figure and the smile
have been replaced by the *Zombie Mum!* That hideous creature which
rises each morning with a gut wrenching growl, the good looks have
become a scowl, the hair now hangs limp without life, the perky
breasts are empty sacks shrivelled and dry, the sparkling eyes are
bloodshot and tired.
The waist and thighs died a horrible death after baby number two,
add another five to that and all that's left is a never-ending stretch mark
to be dumped at sea.
The tight skirts got burnt a long time ago, baggy T-shirts and leggings
are my best friends, the smile if seen, would be lucky to melt an
ice cube, never mind a heart and that ooze has turned into a drip.
Those silly things now warrant little more than a grunt and the
anticipation of life is now 'Yea, OK.' Yes! People I am the
Zombie Mum! I grunt, groan, moan and scream, I'm nothing like
I used to be but I love you all, so perhaps next time before you
run and hide you could try to remember being a *Zombie Mum* isn't
how I want to be.

Doreal Butler

CARS WITH NO FEELINGS

A hedgehog sits on the side of the path
He wonders, can he reach the other side as cars whiz past.

He knows cars have no feelings they just go fast
He decides to make a go for it, ready to make a dash.

His little legs, hurriedly, frantically, he misses a car
Now in the middle, he observes the other side, still so far.

Whoosh! He's got to the other side
As he turns round with two fingers stretched wide.

He scuttles into the grass and into the garden
Away from cars with no feelings, that he had seen.

D Richards

MUMMY

Our little hearts, they missed a beat
When you went out the door
Cos we thought, that we had been bad
And you wouldn't come home no more.

But Daddy sat us on his knee
And told us a little rhyme
About what you are going through
And you will come home feeling fine.

If you get better really quick
And don't get under the weather
We promise to be really good
Today, next week and ever.

Me brother says he'll stop moaning
Well great just fancy that
And me I'll be a good boy
And not a cheeky brat

We'll even clean the toy room up
And make it bright and sunny
'Cos we love you with all our hearts
Our one and only mummy.

Mik Mallett

SEARCHING

Bored and ill at ease I flung myself outside
And strode with irritated tread
Forth into the night.
On hurried feet I sped,
Past the many windows' gleam
That lined my way
And made me seem
An alien cast out by the world
Yet happy in my self-inflicted solitude.
Until at last 'twas there,
The loneliest of all places.
The lofty trees raised gaunt bare
Arms t'ward the boundless sky.
The moon cast brooding shadows,
The wind caressed my brow - while I
Stood still and gazed upon infinity
And felt my irritation die
My spirits rise to meet the sky.

Margaret Parry

DOME OF DOMES

When it comes to making an impression
What will cause you to say, *'Ooh!'*
Will it be the words of a politician,
Or something that ordinary folk do . . .

A 'building', can be quite majestic,
With pinnacles, windows or a tower.
But a 'dome' . . . let's be realistic,
It's the sort of thing put over flowers.

Cathedrals can be topped by a 'dome',
Adding grace and beauty for the eye,
Be it in America, Britain or Rome,
Acceptable structures against the sky.

But the 'Millennium Dome', in the capital,
Such engineering to create a vast space,
The money would have built many a hospital,
With a plaque to commemorate God's grace.

But London must impress the nation,
With exhibits of millennium proportion,
Dwarfing a football stadium, in relation
Temporary exhibition . . . such extortion.

Jenny Major

MOTHER

Basilisk - dead eyes that look on me with hate;
Cold soul from ice-most hell
That brought me - reluctant - to this fate
And watched me - loveless - as I grew,
To watch and ponder on the lack in you.

Unfeeling - how you played on words with me;
Such cold contempt you showed
To one who - unguilty though I be -
Must watch you - loveless as you are -
Stand and pass judgement on the ice in me . . .

Anne Brookes

DEPARTING AN ANGEL

On the inter-city express
I watch the scenery pass. Blinding sun
Reflects these rails on which my iron will runs,
Dividing my destiny and past,
Shining rails stretch to infinity,
Power lines whisper, of immortality . . .

Or hiss like Satan: 'You know it won't last,
How can you, a mere mortal,
Keep this heavenly creature happy?'
So he led me away from the grace of my angel
Who said: 'I can't stay.'

Approaching the terminus,
The driving wheels clattering:
'You can get there on time,'
Like a mantra's rhythm
My mind a new track,
The wheels turning slower, King's Cross at last,
I jump on the platform,
Outrun the demon and it gives its last gasp!

Martin J Mitchell

SPIRIT OF THE SIOUX

Hair the colour of raven's wing
Skin of amber pure
He sits atop his piebald mare
And prays to the Great Spirits there
Head thrown back
Arms flung wide
In the moist and misty prairie morn
Just as day begins to dawn.

He does not ask for riches
No use has he for these
Just the simple things in life
Abundant food, his child, his wife;
His heart is content
His medicine good
All he needs is strength of hand
And freedom in his people's land.

Feet in beaded moccasin
Breechcloth at his waist
He views the wilderness so dear
Knows his destiny lies here
Where eagles soar
And earth meets sky
Land of his forefathers, place of his birth
This is his inheritance
This is his earth.

J Riley

BLACKBERRYING

We usually walked, though it was a long way
And always hot.
Even when we had pennies for the fare
We walked at least a mile beyond the terminus.
A narrow road divided the smooth Links
From the fields of beet awaiting harvest.
Harebells grew by the roadside and ladies' fingers.
At the end of the Links, the road petered out,
A sandy track went a short way, then vanished.

Once arrived, my industrious sisters set to work,
Filling their basins and baskets with blackberries
That squashed between fingers or melted on the tongue.
There were none of those wooden pips
That lurk in hedge berries.

Younger, I was allowed to wander,
First to the little windmill that served no purpose,
And the freshwater dew pond
Where even in August there were tadpoles.
Metallic dragonflies hovered,
Shiny - bright blue and green, their wings gauzy.

Sometimes I made short sorties in the dunes,
Cramming my mouth with fruit and my basket with treasures,
Flowers that wilted before my eyes or
Shells that lost their magic on the journey home.
There were constant cries of, 'Over here!'
As one or another found a more prolific patch,
The fruit was purple, bloomed, low growing,
No heed here for crooked walking sticks.
The better patches were always bettered until,
Tired, hot, sticky, purple with juice,
We went home, where Mum was making pastry.

Ann Harrison

DYING

A grey skin.
Mumbled words
a drifting,
in, out, in again.
Basic needs become
major acts.
A white towel
covering modesty.
Day emerges into night.
Another day
a week passes

Flowers everywhere
a heavy death scent.
Those left waiting
feel suspended
somewhere between
heaven and earth.
Wanting the end
to come,
but afraid to say
goodbyes.

Low voices
as in a waiting room.
A guilty laugh.
Afraid to say
the word
though the word
hangs in the air

as if written
in black capitals.
Fear of what
will come
in time to each and everyone.

Polly Bennison

LIVING FOR LOVE

Born to be wild and free to live, love and the pain
the play when the day ends.
To rest, to nurture teenage dreams to have love, life is
Not what it seems.

To live your hopes, your opinions to love to care for to have
your young
I think the song is nearly sung
it speaks of hope and pain and love
but is your life and your living for love?

Gillian Robson

To The Sad And Lonely

Who is this lonely soul
sitting on a park bench?
Ashen face, drawn,
looking lost, so forlorn.
Only his cigarette for company.
In this world of great speed
greed and evil ways.
Is so destroying to the
poor and weak.
Be with them Lord, as they share
this Christmas with other poor souls,
in the streets and doorways,
park benches, any place of shelter.
Where is the justice
in this money-loving,
fun-loving, crazy world?

Sheila Park

GONE

Going, going, going, gone;
The years behind me now belong.
Like a breath of wind, the blink of an eye,
So the years of my life have slipped quietly by.
Gone are the days when my children were small,
Now they are adults and stand so tall.
I gaze at their photos, that's all that is left,
As I yearn for those years of which I'm bereft.

What now I ask does the future hold?
Only time will tell as the years unfold.
Much reflection on memories past,
To recapture the years that flew so fast.
Now to grow old with aching joints,
Is this where the finger of destiny points?
So onward my body will age and decay,
As the life within slowly ebbs away.
These precious days that run their course
Are moving forward with tremendous force.

When the time is nigh and the soul takes flight,
Onward I'll soar to the heavenly light.
In another time, perhaps another age
The curtain will rise on another stage.
I will take my place and play my part,
In the eternal theatre the performance will start.

Carole Wood

AMBITION

If I were well practised in arts prescient
Future knowledge I'll borrow and consider it to
The present lent
But if such should come to pass
With knowledge from all points of the compass
Then there would be no random chance
And no stake at ventures with a broken lance
I would then tread a chosen path
Each ambition I would stride to the last
But then I would myself condemn
To a life of tedium without end
With no side wind my course to offset
Never a doubt my steadfastness to bereft.

Brian Norman

JUST ANOTHER DAY

Seasons come around then pass
like a breeze upon your face,
silent, then forever on their way.
A trace remains of each
so deep within us all
while time moves into empty space.

With each awakening of the dawn
no welcome for a frown is shown,
as skylarks' song echoes in azure sky.
Golden beams fall as sunshine bright
beckons happiness and joyous life.

Is tomorrow just another day?
Could it ever be for all,
those trumpet sounds, us in song.
Fate leads down ever winding paths
forward we go in merry throng.

No more sadness and goodbyes
leave behind weary mind of past,
look beyond far horizon's brow.
Ride on the winds to distance vast
seek that place where rainbow ends,
and celebrate a life renewed!

H Lewis

MOOD PENITENT

Mid-Lent Sunday
This is the rock on which our stringent disciplines falter
Some to merge with neutral dying winter
Others to live.

Outside the lame wind sharpens its teeth
The pavements are oiled silk. A dismembered newspaper
Threshes the railings like a stranded fish
Cars snick and slur in the puddles

There is a window in your head
Through it I can see your brain marking time like a faulty metronome.
Come to bed - you are tired, and your thoughts, webbed in mine
Are stars shining up through dark water.

We have nothing to give, now.
That alone should not bring us down in flames, or tears.
Watching you, my mind erects its barriers
Only because we have nothing to forgive.

Yet I dismiss your charge of indifference.
The less the rock is revealed
The more it hurts to be flung up against it.

Diana R Cockrill

An Old Man Sighed And Cried

An old man sat on a storm felled tree.
He had sought a quiet place - a private, woodland space.
     The old man sighed, then - cried.

He felt the pain from his tired, worn limbs
And the soreness of his slowing heart.
     The old man cried, then - sighed.

He looked back through the discarded days of his life
And wondered why the living had contained so much strife?
     The old man cried, then - sighed.

Those days floated past as freckled, autumn leaves -
Many of red, ample of brown - just a few of burnished gold.
     The old man cried, then - sighed.

He heard the spring of new-born wails,
Tasting the breast-milk kiss of his infant child.
     The old man cried, then - sighed.

He remembered the hot, passioned love that had conceived that child;
But that love soured cold and bitter with bile.
     The old man cried, then - sighed.

He heard the services in passing praise for the dead -
Friends, relatives now couched forever in their forever beds.
     The old man cried, then - sighed.

He squirmed with frustration through past, covenant laws -
Rules that had hampered the efforts of his natural calls.
     The old man cried, then - sighed.

He had made only the marks allowed the average man,
A few smudged footprints on a vast, open land.
>   The old man cried, then - sighed.

So: he mused on his log - a fallen tree.
What, now, for him is left to be?
>   The old man sighed, then - cried.

William G Thomas

OLD MAN

He awoke with morning pain
Wrinkled worn head bound low
His bones aching and tired brain
Another day began of pain
No more to sleep he weeps
Spoon fed, too tired to eat
He should be able to communicate
Weak unable to stand I held his hand
His body death does he meet
And now I weep.

K Latham

VIOLETS FOR MUM

I can't write a poem
about daffodils
because that's
already been done,
so, I'll write a poem
about violets
and dedicate it
to my mum!

K E Smith

TEETH

When just born and very small,
We haven't any teeth at all.
But then with pain they start to grow,
As any parent will tell you so.

They've walked the floor with a screaming tot,
As cutting teeth really hurts a lot.
Once they are through we chomp away
And for a while they are here to stay.

But don't let them fool you it is for sure,
They wobble, come out to make room for more
Down to our gums again as we grow a new set,
Which are larger and stronger but all that we get.

They have to last for the rest of our time,
So look after yours and I'll look after mine!

Enid Thomas

NOT MY KIDS!

A game of football in the street
Getting caught up with traffic and people you meet
Sneaking in gardens when the ball flies away
Most people grumble, but on with our play.

'I can't understand why they choose to stay here!
When there's a perfect field so very near.'
To be in a gang is most children's aim
Then if windows are broken no one's to blame.

Beulah Thompson

AWAY FROM IT ALL

We went down to Kent the other day,
there was spring in the air and lambs at play.
We sat in the grass with the radio near
and I studied her face so close, so dear
We thought we would find a day of peace
to renew our spirits and find release
But my mind kept turning again and again
to the trouble in Ireland its death and pain.
To our sons who went and fought and died,
to the women who loved and lost and cried.

The sky was misted a delicate blue,
pink and white blossom and air brand new
'Let's find a pub' she said with a smile
'We'll have some lunch and rest a while'
Two voices crept through the smoke and gloom,
reaching my ears across the room
'He killed the old woman, poor little lad,
it wasn't his fault, he wasn't all bad'
'He came from a home without hope or joy'
But it didn't happen when I was a boy.

We went down to Kent and found the sea
and the water sparkled, green and free,
It laughed at the gulls who drift on high,
blissful squeals filling the cloudless sky
We wanted to breathe and run and play,
children again for that lovely day.
Yet still in my mind there lived the thought,
of the wicked world our hands had wrought,
For our little ones, what will be their fate,
is there hope for the future, is it all too late?

Nell Arch

MARY

Mary had some little lambs
Their feet were white as snow
Everywhere that Mary went
The lambs were sure to go
She went up hills down country lanes
Through the valley and the dales
When she turned and looked around
She saw her woolly pals.

Then she saw the farmer coming with his van
She knew where the lambs were going
To be slaughtered and killed by man
And the farmer waiting outside
To take them away in his van
To be made into mincemeat to be put inside a can.

In the factory it's made into sausages and pies
When people eat these sausages
They won't hear the poor lambs' cries
They scoff them down these sausages
What a tasty meal
The ones that eat those sausages
They help towards the kill.

The people should start eating fruit and veg
Which stops you from being ill
When they find it's a tasty meal
Then you find there be no lambs to kill.

Bert Booley

THE BROADWAY (SONG)

Summer fair
but no-one's there
drink ice-cream and lemonade
get a friend and paint their face
but summer's gone
and winter's here
the Broadway and the station master
seem to have disappeared

On the Broadway
the old women talk
about their sons and their love and the size of their guns
and it's nothing to do with me
on the Broadway
the publican cried
she was running away she was talked into staying
and it's all too much for me
on the Broadway
there's no-one around
yet paper runs through and there's so much to do
but there's nothing that I can see
on the Broadway
just passing through
on my Broadway
just passing through

The people talk
the people moan
but they still call
the Broadway their home
she waits around
for a wedding vow
and a wet dream of a man
a man she could never have

A pink dress
an auntie's kiss
a message lost
sure to miss
you take your pills
to ease your pain
but the Broadway seems
to call out your name

Leigh Cullip

AIN'T IT THE TRUTH!

You work like the clappers for your man and your kids
Wash hundreds of saucepans, including the lids,
Hoover the carpets until they are bare
Whilst husband and children stand there and stare,
Then in voices so loud, you could hear them next door
They chorus together 'Mum can we have more
Cornflakes and toast and some marmalade please,'
Whilst I'm in the kitchen shelling the peas!
Get husband out of the door with a kiss
That ought to have been on my mouth but it missed,
It landed instead on the side of my face,
As off to the station my husband did race.
Now get the children all ready for school
Sandwiches packed for each one, I'm no fool,
Cut one slice of bread spread it with jam
Put down the baby outside in the pram,
Collapse into armchair, totally shattered
Wish there were someone to whom I really mattered,
Maybe someday, just one of my crew,
Will say to me 'Mum, we couldn't do without you!'

Maisie Trussler

LAND OF IRE

Christian soldiers they all call them
Fighting for a Christian cause
And off they go to death and glory
Chapters in an age old story
Down the gutters runs the gore, see
The balaclavas hide their sweaty pores
How many more

Loyal just to what they couldn't tell you
Brussels, Dublin, Crown of Jesus Christ
Now he's the bloke who said that loving
Came before the push and shoving
Pardon me, have I said something
A little near the knuckle, not the least
How many more

Bomb blast and bombast will not solve it
Oaths and hypocrisy the same
Where love has met with hate's unreason
Lives are shattered in the treason
Salt unsalted has no season
The divil has your heart, you bloody whore
How many more

How many more, how many more,
How many more, how many more
In the land if Ire,
Mid the blood and the fire
When will they tire
How many more

Martin Harris Parry

THE WONKY VILLAGE

I rode my wonky bike,
all down the wonky lane.
I'm sure it had a wonky wheel,
that's why it's such a pain.

I came to the wonky village
where all the wonky people are
They all had wonky lives I think,
at least; one had a wonky car.

The village church had a wonky spire,
you could see from Wonky Lane.
There, there are two wonky people,
bent over 'gainst the wonky rain.

There were three wonky china shops,
within a wonky mile.
One large delicatessen,
and a computer; with a wonky file.

I said goodbye to the wonky policeman,
as I rode down Wonky Street.
He said 'Cheerio sir,'
as he made his way around his; wonky beat.

T J Elliott

UNTITLED

There is no season that I love best,
but there is beauty when it is winter
and nature takes a rest.
Although it is cold and icy throughout the land,
the frost is sparkling while painted by God's own hand.
He doesn't ask for praise for what we see,
for every garden is treated identically.
There are the patterns on the glass,
which brings a delight when we pass.
We grumble because we feel the cold
and sometimes do not appreciate the patterns untold.
So quietly I thank God above
for bringing this whiteness like a dove.

B J Smith

FAITHFUL FRIEND

Strewn on a bed of lilac with russet leaves
        your pillow
A grassy verge surrounds you, overhung with
        pussy willow.
Oh faithful friend so close the bond for fifteen
        years unbroken
Communicating with our eyes no word having
        need to be spoken.
Such deep devotion over time that grew during all
        those years
I relayed joy and sorrows to your golden
        floppy ears.
As small wet tongue caressed my cheeks and
        wiped away my tears,
No secret betrayed by the lustrous gaze of my
        oft' imparted fears.
But now you are gone, years seven to one
        meant though no telegram from the queen,
You were one of the dearest old ladies that
        this country of ours had yet seen.
But I still chat to you in the garden where you lay
        overhung with gold willow
And I lay alongside you to impart the news
        with my head on your russet leaf pillow.
Oh faithful hound how can I thank you
        for a love over years ever true?
I know one way I can achieve that being the fact
        that I'll certainly never forget you.

Channon Cornwallis

An Ode Of Homage

Let anthems cry out full of humblest of praise
To him, the monarch of all he surveys.
There's nothing more important, I tell you flat,
As a well fed, pampered cat.
In fact it would be most unfair
With mere humans to compare.
'Though motivated by enormous greed
They still remain a superior breed.
Homes are for people, both are for cats,
Make sure they have all the best mats.
Baskets lined with the finest of silk,
Oodles of fish, gallons of milk.
When they enter a room respectfully rise
For we are the menials they rightly despise.
If these precepts you'll follow, they're all very true
Then as an owner purr-haps you will do.

Gordon E Gompers

EQUALITY

Equality is not for me
It's not all it's cracked up to be!
I burned my bra in '63
And off out to work I went
In shoulder pads - one of the boys
We'd manage shops, we'd dig a trench
We'd even work at the fitters' bench
Our children they were all 'minded'
Their latch keys cut all microwave minded
Now thirty years on we're all fed up
No jobs for the boys - the girls have got 'em
Together with the cooking and the washing
We are all worn to a frazzle
Family life's gone down the drain
Let the male chauvinist rule again

Lin Fortune

WAITING FOR THE TRAIN

How white the may!
And how it emulates the lazy high flown clouds.
The back cloth pines and shaded paler ranks
Of hazel, sycamore and ash
Hide my first chiffchaff, who reiterates his claim.
Bright yellow ragwort, uninvited, stands
Revelling in sunshine on the gritty bank
And all along the rusticating track,
While here and there blue comfrey flowers unfurl
To match the brilliant sky.

Bird song and may scent - all in harmony
Until a cheerful chatterbox intervenes
And sweet but alien perfume falls on the summer air.

Beryl Jenkyn

FROST IN MOONLIGHT IN THE COUNTRYSIDE

Valleys covered with tiny frost stars
        on a winter's midnight,
In the freezing golden moonlight,
Crystallised forests are magical wonderlands
        of ice,
Their frozen beauty glowing icily nice,
Moonbeams caress the sculptural ice crystal
        flowers,
In the bewitching moonlit hours,
Hedgerows encrusted with frost crystals are
        a sparkling sight,
In the windless wintry moonlight,
The icy beauty of the fields and farms,
Glistening with their frosty charms,
Jack Frost has sprinkled tiny twinkling frost
        stars everywhere,
In the icy moonlit air,
Leaving an enchanted spell of frozen starry
        white,
In the countryside in the moonlight.

E Jamieson

THE BUMBLEBEE

Have you ever watched the bumblebee
Flit from flower to flower?
I could watch that bumblebee
Hour after hour.
His downy body of black and yellow,
To me he's such a decent fellow.

He works so hard to pollinate,
So fellow man for heaven's sake
Don't swat the little bumblebee,
He works so hard for you and me.

Where would we be without him,
I just fear to dread.
The flowers would die and wither,
Never raise their colourful heads.

When you see the bumblebee
Just you stop and think,
It's one of life's small miracles,
Don't make the bee extinct.

L James

POLYOXYCARBONATE

Polyoxycarbonate,
Goodness knows what that would make!
It just sprang into my head
Whilst I was out a-walking!

Miximystotoperene,
Goodness knows what that could mean!
It just sprang into my head
Whilst I was out a-walking!

Antiproductphoxide,
Goodness knows I really tried
To stop it springing into my head
Whilst I was out a-walking!

Uprofoxidhydroclone,
Goodness me it goes on and on.
The words spring into my head
Whilst I am out a-walking!

Systomatopuroned,
Goodness me, how is that said?
Why do these words spring to mind?
Whilst I am out a-walking!

Thorinexiturnastout,
Goodness knows what that's about!
How do these words spring to mind?
Whilst I am out a-walking!

Homeositeolockthedoor,
Goodness me I'll say no more!
A cup of tea springs to mind
Now I am not a-walking!

Eugenia Sanderson

THE SHADOW

The shadow that follows me,
Looks just like me.
In fact he never runs away,
He's always right beside me.
When it's lunchtime he shoots up tall,
But when it's night time he's not there at all.
He always plays beside me,
When the sun is out of bed.
He always sticks around me,
I'd like another playmate instead.

Charlotte Jacobs

LONDON/RAMSGATE

London

On grey stone steps assemble nicotine
addicts pulling seasonal weather.
A car pulls out, speeds up, overtakes,
slows down, indicates, parks.

On every grey stone step assembles every
nicotine addict pulling seasonal weather.
An industry of cars pull out, accelerate,
overtake, slow down, indicate, park.

Ramsgate

This moment caught by my fingertips
I had a hot coffee drink at my lips
beside bobbing boat bay's crying child
wearing a baseball cap forming puddles
on Thanet's isle beneath screeching choir
at a dock of the bay pavement table cafe
watching salt water teardrops of told off
drop off silently lashed thick eyeballs.

Lawrance-Marc Richards

RUSH HOUR

It's 7 o'clock! The alarm goes off.
I jump in the shower. I look for the towel
and then I remember it's still in the dryer.

I limp to the bedroom. I open the curtains:
no rain or snow or blustery showers.

I dress very quickly. I look in the mirror and
with horror I see the Walt Disney tie
doesn't go with my style.
I look at the socks: one pink and one orange.

It's 7.20! I turn on the kettle. I go to the fridge
and soon realise the milk is all finished.

I go to the door and as I step out the alarm goes off.
It's 7 o'clock!

I open my eyes and happily smile.
It was a bad dream and the sun is now shining.

Franca Gatto

SILENT LOSS

When affection has gone
and the understanding
of its value is lost

So too, is the relationship.

Reds

UNION

Beside a swaying lunar tide,
opening to life's ancient ebb and flow,
we enter the secret chamber;
the alchemical furnace within
our deep heart's core.

Embracing the undertow our bodies,
minds and souls open to the
pull of ocean, open to the presence
of the one.

And the earth our home
sails, afloat in the void,
an ark amid teeming shoals
of stars and an ocean unfathomed.

Alan Davies

THE DOG

I sit alone and wonder why
My owner's gone, it makes me cry
Oh why, oh why did she leave me
Without even a bone for tea?

I pace and dig and dig and pace
I have to get out of this lonely place
I bark and howl and scratch and chew
Is this what I am meant to do.

The time drags by I'm so alone
I only want a loving home
Instead I sit here full of woe
Why she left I'll never know.

But wait is that a noise I hear
I turn around and lift my ear
Oh joy it is I've company
And in the door there turns a key.

Oh you are a naughty pup
You've torn the mat and chewed it up
You make such noises, I don't know
Why you're carrying on so.

It is all right, I bark with glee
My mistress's not deserted me
I know I really shouldn't moan
As I was only left at home.

Linda Palmer

ALONE

A solitary bird flying high up in the sky
A solitary bird flying way up high
What is he looking for, what does he seek?
Why is that lonesome call coming from its beak?

He's flying all alone and looking very free
Could it be he's happier, happier than me
Maybe he's found what I am looking for
I think he has the key to open up the door

Happiness will always be just a state of mind
But freedom is harder, much harder to find
But that solitary bird flying high upon the wing
Has the secret of true freedom, so listen to him sing

Sheila Trim

THE BLUES

Don't tell me who's died and who's sick
Don't tell me I'll die if I smoke!
Don't moan or complain again and again
Goodbye to the sadness - *good health*
Don't moan 'cause it's raining
And the sky isn't blue
They'd be glad of the rain in the dessert
Just give to the needy and not to the greedy
Be good and look after yourself!

M Story

IT WAS THEN I DREAMED

It was then I dreamed
Of small, furry hamsters
Sleeping in the daytime
Awake in the night time
I cleaned cages
Sawdust and bedding
Water to drink
Toys to play with
It was then I dreamed of hamsters
Small furry hamsters
Playing in their houses
Eating food and treats.

Samantha Whiting (11)

THANK YOU

Thank you for giving us friendships
And bags of fish and chips
Thank you for giving us money
And bread and jam and honey
For skies so blue
And the morning dew
For sea and sand
And the village band
For dogs and cats
And balls and bats
For books and toys
And girls and boys
For chalks and pens
And chicks and hens
For birds and bees
And the summer breeze
For flowers and leaves
And leafy trees
For seaside shells
And Christmas bells
For cosy socks
And pretty frocks
For fairy lights
And bikes and kites
For the moon and stars
And chocolate bars
For a life so full of lovely things
Thank you God for everything

Ruth Bell

THE WORLD AROUND US

The world is full of people
Of every race and creed,
Masses of humanity
In which there is much need.
Disasters strike - like earthquakes.
Floods and hurricanes,
And thousands die as homes and goods
Are swept away by rains.
There is much greed in the world today
And much more poverty too,
The charities all do their best
With what they are able to do.
It's been like this since ancient times
As the Holy Bible states,
These happenings are nothing new
But are they what man creates?
We tamper with the environment,
Pollution fills the air -
Can all the disasters be partly our fault?
It's time to take stock and take care.

Freda Searson

KEY TO HAPPINESS

If you've got a friend you've got happiness,
And I certainly know this is true,
Just pick up a pen and write from your heart,
Then your moments will never be blue!
Speak as you feel and chatter away
Till all of your 'nightmares' have gone;
Lift up the phone and you'll ne'er be alone,
And pleasure and joy will be one!
Get in touch with the Lord at least once an hour,
Tell Him you love Him and care,
Then the thoughts you have had, which at times were so bad,
Will seem like a breath of fresh air!

Sharon Howells

FIELD OF SLEEP

Who could imagine what would happen, if the people in the field of
sleep would stir and wake, to reveal their dreams and needs?
Unfulfilled dreams that never were, that never inhaled the fresh air of
reality.

Should we sit and listen and just try to understand, to grasp what might
have been and still might be?
But can a sleep that has no end reveal the unknown feeling it hides
beneath a blanket of earth?

The field will welcome all and allow the slumber to continue regardless
of age, colour or creed.
If the dreams were granted their freedom, let loose on a fragile world,
who would care?
Would changes be made as the dreams turned to reality, as the field of
sleep released the emotions of lost people.

People that will never age, people whose dream will not be heard or
turned into reality.
Just imagine, just try to imagine.

Julian Hackett

ANNIVERSARY DAY

They'd had their ups and they'd had their downs
Though the joys they remembered exceeded the frowns:
And now it was their *special* day
Gifts, cards and flowers came their way
Today's memories would sparkle for evermore
Diamond weddings don't come often, that's for sure
'Sixty years with one man - how could that be?'
Asked the girl in the card shop 'Better her than me!'
But when God's at the centre, the marriage is strong
Love rules - and the years don't seem any too long.

Muriel I Tate

QUIETLY

I live alone, but lonely I do not get
because in my life I have God who does not forget,
at quiet times I listen for what He has to say
and give a prayer of thanks to Him every day.

I live alone, but am surrounded by friends
every day I pray for someone who depends,
on my prayers of faith, healing and hope
knowing they have someone to call on they can cope.

I live alone, and throughout my life
I've called on God at times of doubt and strife,
He never leaves me although sometimes I stray
God the Father looks over me each and every day.

I live alone, except for God and Jesus His son
they know all about my thoughts and what I've done,
so thank you Father God Almighty
I pray at the end of each day, quietly.

George Reed

THE DALMATIAN CAT

I'm white with spots of black
Now and then I visit a friend
She told Big Tabby off
And saved me from attack.

It's quite a while since I have been
But my leg is in plaster
How can I get through the fence?
What a trial - I cannot go any faster.

Well here I am - look at me
I've come for sympathy
Now you know why I've been away
Restricted - house bound until today.

Now my plaster's off, I'm here again
Just to let you see my leg is better
I can run and play and climb a tree
Thanks to a good bone setter.

Myrtle E Holmes

MAGIC MOON WHITE

She is there by my side
she knows
she won't let me cry,

everytime she comes
and purrs a soft song,
a lullaby

her cuddles are the best
she makes everything right,
she's my champion.

She's the best,
cat is a woman's best friend.

Sylvie Wright

A Stay In Hospital

When I was about six years old
And my throat had been sore quite a lot,
The doctor said I needed my tonsils out
Whether I agreed with him or not.

I was next shown round the hospital ward
To get me used to the place,
I wasn't having that I remember saying
With tears streaming down my face.

The nurses gave me a doll to hold,
I threw it on the floor, I was so mad,
No way was I going to stay in there,
I was going home with my mum and dad.

On turning round I saw them leaving,
They were disappearing through the door,
The nurses tried to quieten me
As I lay screaming on the floor.

In the end I settled down
And had my tonsils out next day,
Things weren't as bad as I'd imagined,
I enjoyed the ice-cream anyway!

Joan A Anscombe

REFLECTION IN A PUDDLE

Months of hype about the eclipse
This subject spoken on everyone's lips
Media coverage at saturation point
Hippies in Cornwall smoking a joint
I closed the curtains so my cats couldn't see
The major event that was about to be
People outside holding bits of card
All standing like lemons in the backyard!
Grown men peering into a puddle
Everyone seemed in a bit of a muddle
But it didn't grow dark and dogs didn't bark
The buds kept on singing - even the lark
The moon blocked the sun - so what if it did
The eclipse went down here just like a damp squid
People will chant, dogs may pant
And the crazy amongst us reassure a plant!
The eclipse of the sun will make some nerves jangle
For the next time we'll view it
From a different angle!

Christine Anne Storer

ALONE

I see an old man in his garden that he's tended for years,
He's all alone just feeding the birds.
Sometimes the kids come round,
Sometimes they don't but he's never alone.
He thinks of the happiness he has known when he
                                    wasn't alone,
The love of his wife he'll never forget,
Can't understand the illness that struck and shattered
                                    their happiness.
Memories and pictures are all that's left
To remind him of their happiness.

David Frost

MY FRIEND

As we stood and said goodbye
My tears began to fall
We wanted you to stay
But we knew you had to go
Gone from my sight
But not from my heart
Your memories are mine to keep
Now we are apart.

Ella Wright

LIFE NAVIGATION THEORY

The universe cloaks us;
Earth, a small sphere,
Placed among a scattered riot of twinkling stars.
This coat of gyrating gems somehow,
Leads the lives, forges the fortunes,
Of inmates held, tight within its sparkling bars.
Or so it is said.

For exchange of practice for money;
Inmates, ones that choose to trick a mind,
And coax a brain to ill-perceive.
Read Horoscopes - heaven sent con,
Birth signs, star charts, maps of the cosmos,
State a victim's future, vague enough to believe.
Subtle cues to feed the head.

The accomplished astrologer;
Chants utterances of commonplace insecurities - speculations,
Relying on life's everyday occurrence to conjure an obscure prediction.
With wealth induced self-delusion he,
Teases the senses of feeble captives, with border truths,
Casting every doubt of what could be superstition.
So the map of life is read.

Christine Rooth

SMOKING

My dear husband Paul has given up smoking
Yes, I too at first thought he must be joking
Many times in the past he's tried it before
The only thing that happened was he smoked even more

But no, not this time, he's determined to crack it
He promised me that he has bought his last packet
He really did mean it he's done very well
With the help of some patches of Nicotinell

It's made such a difference, there's no smell of fags
And as for the money, well now we've got bags
We've both changed our cars and been abroad twice
And there's no smell of fags, it really is nice

He's kept to his word and hasn't had one since
But now he's addicted to extra strong mints

I Jenkinson

SILHOUETTES

An old man standing on the street
Holding a pad, black cardboard sheet.
Shiny scissors in wrinkled, brown hands,
Snipping and turning, leaving long paper bands.

Ladies of fashion look demure and blush,
Pose for a minute with momentary hush.
While fingers and scissors with dexterity twist,
Then the profile is there, black and crisp.

The children stare at his strange attire
In a shirt badly faded, once red as fire.
Blue baggy trousers, patched and torn,
Shoes far too big, shabby and worn.

A bearded face, twinkling blue eyes,
Keen yet kindly, knowing and wise.
Noting each contour of the faces before him,
Some smiling, some mocking, others silent and grim.

A policeman stands with patient air
As the scissors flash with infinite care.
A child's face was there, cut paper thin
With turned up nose and rounded chin.

The crowd moves away, the old man turns,
Shuffles along alone and spurned.
Searching for faces, beautiful and delicate
To capture forever on a black silhouette.

Lois Burton

FOOL'S GOLD

A sudden rush of hot, stale air overwhelmed
greeting the chosen few,
eager and expectant, a small hole,
light was tempted through.

Reaching out from the darkness, shone from within, a small child's
                                    voice whispered, 'to enter is to sin,'
the guardians and spirits warned of evils entangled inside,
yet in fate's face they scoffed, mysteriously
they all died.

The boy king's royal burial site had already been plundered
by ancient thieves,
all of whom perished to the curse that none throughout
                                    time believes.

When the seals were broken no-one noticed that outside day had
                                    turned to night,
those fabulous treasures would not be yielded by the other side
to mortals without a fight.

Fabulous wealth, fame and fortune, so hypnotic the greed, danger
and misfortune awaits eagerly in their lair
as they stepped through into another world their ancestors
awoke with a cry of despair.

Michael Hartshorne

ON GARDENS

The garden is not
An inspiration anymore.
Now that I am alone,
It's just another big chore.
It is not the work that I detest
And I always try my best,
But the annoyance of it be, is
What else I could be doing,
Were I free?

When will I have time
To sit on the swing?
There goes the 'phone again,
Will I let it just ring?
Where get the time,
To go and just sit,
Admire the view,
Read a few pages from a mag,
Listen to the bees and birds,
Enjoy the warmth?
I just quit.

Mariè Brown

COVER ME

Cover me with flowers
so I may taste their sweetened scent
as I moulder away my final hours
I may inhale their coloured breath
that extols my death
and praises the very end of me
of whom I used to be, so You may mourn
and bury these rotten bones, I used to own
but now discard for things anew
for places only dreamed by mere man
because I can, and because I may
so I shall travel amongst the stars
as my body rots, I'll soar so far
and ride astride the solar winds
yet always, my heart must here remain
tied here to you, because of the things you do
and because of the flowers
that once covered me, it's where I must be
and though I may fly and go, I must always return
right back to where we're born
and still linger, even now, waiting eternally,
for the flowers to wither and die
and still as each year passes
you cover my ashes, with flowers anew
that bind me, here to you, and tie me here
though you cannot see the tear
that falls from this terrible face
yet it may water them flowers
where at my graveside they grace
So yeah! cover me with flowers! but then let me go!
forever, for now I am gone
I loved you, ya know!

Jeff Mitchell

THE PIT

The pits are all closed now
The wheels they are still
Grass cover the ground that once was the pit hill
Cages that lowered men deep into the ground
Lanterns and helmets no more to be worn
Snap tin, knee pads most of them torn
Dark roadways are quiet, no sound of a horn

The old pit men have gone, time moves so fast
Pit ponies and't holster are things of the past
An era has gone, some good times, some bad
Nothing's the same as when dad was a lad
A miner's life was all he knew
When a pit closes what was he to do?

Ann Quibell

THE SEASONS

Spring is here once again
There are buds on all the trees
The daffodils and narcissus
Are dancing in the breeze

After springtime summer follows
Now is the time for the swallows
They fly from abroad every year
And go back again when autumn is here

The next season is autumn
And the squirrels stock up for the wintertime
Ready for when the days are cold
The leaves on the trees are brown and gold

Winter comes and brings the snow
The glistening trees are all aglow
Children sledge yet do not seem to tire
I just like to sit by a nice log fire

May Ward

BE STILL

A moment of your time, is all I ask of you,
Do not speak concentrate, for words are
weak; and commonplace,
Feel the earth beneath your feet, touch
the things you love.
See the strongest, tallest tree, and the
stars above.
Listen to the sounds, echoing far and near,
watch the children play, innocents have no fear,
Hear the rain, as it softly falls, and the
bell's lonely call
Open your eyes and your mind, there
are treasures all around.
So a moment's silence if you please,
to smell the flowers, to feel, to see.
Take that moment, to stand and stare,
in case tomorrow isn't there.

I Welch

EMMA LOUISE

It seems like only yesterday,
I held you in my arms,
Recall, with so much pleasure
All your childhood charms,
Watched you make your grades at school,
Dance your way through college,
The world now opens up for you
To pass on all your knowledge,
For me, you're truly special
I pray for you each day,
May the good Lord bless and keep you,
And guide you through life's way.

Gramps

Tom Grocott

GOD CREATED EVERYTHING

Our Lord God
God of the universe
You made the heavens
You made the earth
You created everything.

Lord God
You made the birds
You gave them wings to fly
High above the earth
High in the sky
You created everything.

Our Lord God
You made the fish
They swim in the sea
Some You made
To feed me
You created everything.

Our Lord God
You made the animals
To roam the earth
You breathed Your breath
Into man, gave him birth
You created everything.

Doreen Swann

BAGNALL VILLAGE

Bagnall stands high upon a hill,
I was born not far from the village,
I bet a good many can remember still.
I was a bit of a lad
And my name is Bill.

The church stands pointed towards the sky,
A lot of my relatives are buried in the church yard.
Some passed away because they were ill,
Others died as they were getting old,
On a winter's day it does get rather cold.

In the summer when the sun does shine,
You could call in The Stafford Arms Public House,
For a beer, a snack, or a glass of wine
And drown your sorrows, before closing time.

I've spent some happy moments on the village green,
As a boy with my friends, some capers? Not to be seen,
Although, now I'm getting haggard, old and grey,
I can very nearly remember that very first day.

I met a lovely lass, we were both thirteen,
We went out with each other for over a year.
Then when we left school we went our own separate ways,
Now after fifty three years, we've met again
And we hope we'll be together for many, many days.

I haven't been to Bagnall Church for quite some time
But I've remembered it and the green in this little rhyme.
Perhaps, I'll visit the church one day soon
And recall what happened, underneath the moon.

William Jebb

FRIENDSHIP

A good friend in life is something to be treasured,
Their trust and loyalty just cannot be measured.
They share your worries and share you fears,
They join in your laughter and with you shed a few tears.
This friend you have, has a heart of gold
And your best-kept secrets will never be told.
If sadly this friend is no longer there,
They've taught you a lesson in life,
They've taught you to care.
This friend isn't your cousin, your sister, or brother,
I'm talking about, your own loving mother.

Margaret Clowes

GET IN TOUCH

Get in touch with your feelings,
Unlock the door -
Have you chained them up evermore?
There is no law
To keep them chained up bruised and sore.
Get in touch with your feelings.

Get in touch with your feelings,
You're stronger now.
Stop falling back on 'sometime', 'somehow',
Discarding pain,
Doesn't have to mean you'll hurt again.
Get in touch with your feelings.

Get in touch with your feelings,
Open your heart.
Trample that wall that keeps you apart,
You need not give
A single thing you don't want to give.
But time's moving fast; it's time to live!
Get in touch with your feelings.

Sylvia Anne Lees

THINKING WHAT TO WRITE

A letter through the post one day
I'd found upon the floor,
Lying there, looked slightly bent
Propped up against the door.

I expected it was prodded through
Jerked with a forceful shove,
Falling freely through the air
From our letter box above.

As I opened the envelope's seal
A little yellow letter,
Reading through it carefully
Then saw it couldn't get much better.

£10,000 in cash awards
For something I loved to do,
Write poetry and get it published
I hoped . . . could this make two?

So I got scribbling that very night,
Lots of thoughts, but one I'd missed,
The letter I'd got and then I thought
'What would they think of this?'

Beth Simpson (14)

MY SECRET COVE

There's a tiny secret cove
Which has a golden sandy shore,
With lots of lovely rock pools, whilst
Overhead squalling seagulls soar.

Hemmed in by cliffs and rocks, I feel
So happy and contented there.
The waves are lapping round my feet
I really am without a care.

Perfect peace, no one to disturb
My thoughts of times gone by.
When galleons and pirate ships
Sailed passed with banners high.

I dream of silvery blue tailed
Mermaids lying on the rocks.
Basking in the noon day sun and
Combing their long golden locks.

Of long ships with oars held high
And smugglers with their contraband.
Lord Nelson with the full Armada,
Well equipped and fully manned.

Oh dear, it's time to say farewell
To this dear place I love so dear.
But I'll be back to savour more
A little later in the year.

Joyce Wakefield

BOLBERRY

A thick grey mist reached from horizon to horizon
Voices were hushed feeling the clammy air.
It was not long, for almost at once
Sunset rose from every side - orange, pink, palest yellow.

Overhead the grey dusk remained, a darker circle rushed
Across the sea, this the penumbra of the moon.
The clouds still did not break, hiding the eclipse.
They would not part thickly hiding the view.

So near and yet not in our vision.
Perhaps totality could be seen in the neighbouring bay
Maybe the promontory behind. Low conversation began
The sky lightened. The eerie dusk dispersed.

Jane England

SUZIE SPROCKET

My name is Suzie Sprocket
I had a tickly pocket
My grandad said I was a scamp
Which is better than being a tramp!

My name is Suzie Sprocket
I had a tickly pocket
It was where my grandad tickled me
And I laughed and chuckled with glee!

My name is Suzie Sprocket
I had a tickly pocket
Although I am now twenty-three
I remember how it tickled me

My name is Suzie Sprocket
I am old and have no tickly pocket
I remember dear grandad more and more
As he tickled me to the core.

Jack Purdom

THE CANAL

Fields of red ridged soil, like silent soldiers stand.
Lush meadows green and filled with flowers.
Hawthorn hedges with tightly curled buds,
Ash and willow, languid and graceful.
This is countryside for which we should be grateful.

Through this beauty and splitting it apart,
Is an artery which feeds its heart.
The canal was built long ago,
It does not wind, it does not bend,
But it is straight from end to end.

The locks are hills which barges climb,
To enter and leave is a thief of time,
What does it matter, what do we care?
We are here in God's clear and special air,
Slow and time consuming is the pace,
This is a journey not a race.

Twinkling windows shining bright,
Of a pub, beckons and calls,
Come inside, cease your ride, enjoy our comforts
When our doors you open wide.
Tarry a while, drink our beer, eat from our table,
Then outside you go and untie the cable.
Start the engine, thump, thump, thump.
Careful, careful, into the bank you must not bump.

Along the still and tranquil water you glide,
Passing the ducks and swans by your side,
The sun sets red up in the sky,
The canal is still as still can be.
The time has come to stop for tea.
The day has ended the air is chill,
Tie up the barge, make it secure,
Put down your head for sleep so pure.

Carl Kemper

GRANDFATHERS' SONG

The world is changing
The sky is darkening
The winds move more swiftly
A storm is coming
A storm we cannot withstand
Rising in the east
With power and force
Guided from the south
With light and righteousness
Encouraged from the north
With wisdom and foreknowledge
To the west
To break the shadow
To relieve the earth
To give back the growth
This is not a force of destruction
This is a force of life
So stand in the rain
Stand and let the life
Flow back into you

Ian Davies

SHADES OF GREY

Hate not the morning all shades of grey,
for earth is preparing,
     recharging her batteries,
     having a little rest.

turn not in scorn,
at the morn, all shades of grey,
for she is awaiting the birth of spring,
when colours bright,
will set alight,
morning skies of red and gold,
pastures green,
daisies white,
yellow sun,
deep purple nights.

earth needs her morn of shaded grey,
to prepare for spring,
that's on its way.

begrudge her not this restful time,
forgive her,
if she feels a little down.
we all have days of shaded grey,
while we wait for spring to come our way.

Jacqueline Claire Davies

MY WONDERFUL WORLD

I often sit and wonder
At the splendour of this world,
My thoughts do often wander
Like a flag that's just unfurled,
I see a tree in blossom,
All dressed in pink and white,
Clasping the sun to its bosom,
It is a wonderful sight.

I hear the song of the birds on high,
I see them wing their way in the sky,
The squirrels with their quaint bushy tails,
The silver thread of the slow moving snails,
The robin with his breast so red,
Comes a begging for his crust of bread,
I feel the rain softly touch my face,
I know this world is a wonderful place.

I meet my friends each day I live,
I know this life has so much to give,
I take things for granted, each day I live,
The pleasures, the sorrows, the sunshine, the rain,
There is so much I'd give, so much to gain,
It's a wonderful world just the same.
A life of contentment, a life full of grace,
It's a wonderful, it's a wonderful place.

D Hampton

RAGS OR RICHES, SLAVES OR MASTERS

Oh what am I supposed to do
But walk on the streets in my rags and slippers.

Oh what am I supposed to do
But give my spare change to man,
So he too, can walk on the streets in his rags and slippers.

Oh what am I supposed to feel
But anger towards the plastic people around me.

Oh how am I supposed to feel
But like a bed of weeds next to a garden full of roses.

Oh what am I supposed to think
But that only the rich and beautiful go ahead in life.

Oh what am I supposed to think
But that I have to be one or the other to be high on life.

Since I have neither
I will seek medical advice from *Cosmopolitan.*
Then I too will be beautiful
And thus go down the stairs to the pits of hell
And become rich like the others.

Oh what am I supposed to do
But dress, look and act like the plastic people around me.

Oh what am I supposed to do
But keep my spare change for myself
And let man have no rags and slippers to walk on the streets with.

'There's enough for everyone's needs,
But not enough for everyone's greed.'
Mahatma Ghandi.

N B Dahl

To My Son

September morning silent - still
The soft grey mist shrouding the hill
The dew is heavy, there's a nip in the air
Bejewelled spider webs are everywhere
The ripe apples fall the horse chestnuts too
The mist is now lifting, I look at the view
The sun is rising ever so slow
Bathing the earth to a warm mellow glow
I do love September - always remember
It was just such a day
When you were born
A beautiful, golden September morn

Olive Allgood

QUANTUM LEAP

Let's leap in time, to days of yore,
When life was then a lasting chore.
Communication by pen or mouth,
Transport by loco, shunting south.

Coal sent by narrow barge,
Clothes plain, hats too large?
Food from free range hens,
Vegetables grew immense!

Wealth was for the privileged few,
Aristocrats with a conservative view.
The poor lived by tiresome means,
Working long hours in their teens.

Miners toiled in closet tombs,
Like working bees in honeycombs.
Their icon, the pit head mound,
Above their heads on solid ground.

Family values held in high esteem,
Justice instant, no in-between.
Quantum theory is pros and cons,
Heritage for our sons.

Alan Dawes

WE

We met as strangers
And then as friends
Listened and learned
Searched and found
Talked and touched
Kissed and cried
Loved and lied
We knew what we wanted
If only we'd tried
Telling each other
How we felt inside
Forget the ego
Forgot the pride
Forget it
Goodbye

B R B George

SPRING IN ENGLAND

Spring is now arriving,
With its beauty and its grace,
Calling to the year's first flowers,
To show their timid face.
The swallows are returning,
And the buzzy bees do hum,
While the other birds sing merrrily
Of summer days to come.

For where in all this wide, wide world
With climates cold and warm
Is there any place like England
With its simple graceful charm?
Its leafy lanes and meadows,
Its placid lakes and streams,
Where artists sit for hours and hours
With painting and their dreams.
For England is the home of spring,
And hope and happiness,
An emerald in a sea of blue,
Amidst this world of stress.

B Ruffles

KING EDWARD THE SEVENTH'S MEDALS
(1901 - 1910)

The gaylord King awarded four*
As his short Reign proceeded to
Its own untimely and cirrohotic end,
Bereft of personal gain or friend.
Yet gallant lords and soldiers tried
To defend the Empire's bordered pride.

Setbacks there were, sun-blistered men
Marched valiantly to staunchly extend
His Majesty's and God's own field
Through blistering rock-strewn barren ground,
Where ethnic traits no succour yields
And hostile fiends refused the Crown.

Youth, as to every Nation blessed
Comes forth, in its own time unpressed,
And willingly serves both God and King
In campaigns brave but oft unseen.

Any Nation's life, its Government's too,
Depend on individuals who do
Their beckoning in their time of need,
Unhindered and not short in speed,
          providing energy and will,
To serve all others with good not ill.
Remembering that tomorrow's gain
          feeds everyone despite the pain
Of seeing some who pass you by then fail,
'Cos human frailty prevails.

So God sets His own standards for all to seek
And makes life achievable for the meek.
He knows that our lives are emboldened
In our present World so real.
We find that King Edward's medals
Were a reward for tenacity and zeal.

The India Medal - 1900
  The Ashanti Medal - 1900
  The King's South Africa Medal (Anglo-Boer War) 1901-2
  The Africa General Service Medal (1902-56) for Kenya

Brian Harris

THE PARTING

My heart is heavy as I travel on,
Life seems empty since you have gone,
Our wonderful memories of yesterday
Travel with me on my way.
Sometimes I feel your presence near
And long just for your voice to hear.
Daily I tread my pathway of life
With meetings, partings, joys and strife,
Time alone will release this pain
Till one day in heaven we'll meet again.

S M Bush-Payne

FOREVER YOURS

On a warm summer's evening hand in hand
We strolled barefoot across the sand.
Two people so much in love, for all to see,
Living our lives only for each other, just you and me.

Whisperings of love as we tenderly kiss,
Lost in each other, I recall those feelings of bliss.
Our eyes expressing our deep, meaningful love,
Silhouettes against the sun setting in the sky above.

That evening you asked me to be your wife,
To be yours forever, for the rest of your life.
I still treasure that moment when I said 'I will,'
Thirty years down life's path I adore you still.

Maggy Copeland

PEOPLE

Some people are happy, some people are sad,
Some people are good, some decidedly bad.
Some people are clever and many are not,
Some people want everything others have got.
Some people can paint, play piano or sew,
Some people have homes, others nowhere to go.
We are all different I've heard people say,
Perhaps in the end it is better that way.

M M Watts

SPIDER MAN

Well out of sight spider man spies
Having created a web site of lies
Now sits waiting for coming of flies

Spider man always lays a good bait
And if a fly is emeshed in his web
It may be too late to make an escape

If a fly likes a flutter it must be wise
When the bait looks too good to be true
A fly needs to fly with wide open eyes

With a spider man hiding in a web site
A fly must be aware, with a bait comes a snare
And spider man always looks out for his bite

Fate does not favour the unwary fly
Spider man springs into sight for a kill
And spider man will suck any fly dry

K W Benoy

THE JOURNEY

A silent man who homeward bound must go
leaves his journey printed in the snow.
Stacatto steps make crunching music from the ground
and breaks cold silence which is all around.
Peaked, pinched his face now all aglow
from lips, a stream of vaporous air does blow.

Soon his cottage looms in sight
from latticed windows shines a light.
Reflecting on earth's mantled snow
like tiny diamonds all aglow.
With glistening beauty they do vie,
stars studded in a velvet sky.

Now his steps increase in pace
as to his cottage he does race.
Arriving at the stout oak door
clogged snow is stamped off on the floor.
Inside he steps, his one desire
welcoming wife by burning fire.

E L G Holmes

THE DYING TIMES

As the abbey stood so proud,
The 300 years of hard labour is put to shame
As Whitby Abbey is turned to flame.
No more silence, no more peace,
There is just screaming and shouting and more to tell,
But the roof of the abbey tumbled and fell.
The nave is burning and is full of light
And it is left to die alone, fearful and bright.

In the rush a lady drops her screaming baby,
That has just been blessed.
It will not make it through the long, choking night.
Outside the monks are chanting,
Begging for the survival of their home.
Their tries are doomed to failure,
As there is *nothing* that can save
Their pride, not now
Not ever.

Kate Boothroyd (12)

EXPLANATIONS

I had to explain to my children and find the right words to say
Tell them their father still loved them although he had gone away
       I told my daughter
I heard the shock but her scorn was there as the questions began
We always thought you were clever but you could not keep your man
       I told my son
Such a look of pain which I could not ease and then a deepening cry
You know my new plane we were starting to build now it will never fly
Then living alone I kept asking why did our dreams end in strife?
We were really in love when we married and it was meant for life
Our joinings were always a wonderful gift to show that we really cared
How good were the talks so grave to start then to end in the jokes
                   we shared
Slowly the change was coming, living together had lost its charm
I know that I loved my husband, did not think he would cause me harm
He told me about this other love and said he would have to go
But he had not meant this to happen and knew it would be a blow
She was quite young and so lovely and soon he was under her spell
He would do all he could to help us and hoped I would wish him well
So this was the end of our marriage, I did not know who to blame
It began with all our best wishes to end it was such a shame
I had to be brave for the children you see
But harder it was to be brave for me.

May Walker

SOMEWHERE OUT THERE

Where do lonely hearts weep?
For their place I do not know.
Is it where lost souls sleep?
For that's where I eventually go.
I think I know of it,
It's where all the lost tears must flow.
Probably by a river,
Where the coldest of winds do blow.

M Murphy

MAJESTIC ROSE

So lovely is the majestic rose
That high upon the trellis grows
In many beautiful coloured pastel shades
Dispersing sweet perfume as the sunlight fades

Eagerly visited by the bees and butterflies
As the early morning sun begins to rise
And flowers still glistening with early morning dew
Greet a new day with their fragrant colourful hue

Yes the rose is truly a wondrous sight
With its pastel shades of red, yellow, pink and white
Enhancing your garden as it blossoms and grows
Truly a wonder of nature is the majestic rose

Anthony Carlin

TWELVE

I woke up when the clock struck twelve,
I cried, I couldn't help myself.

I watched the clock as it struck one,
I can't believe that you are gone.

I watched the clock as it struck two,
beside my bed is a picture of you.

I watched the clock as it struck three,
you're no longer here with me.

I watched the clock as it struck four,
you won't be coming home any more.

I watched the clock as it struck five,
you are gone, I'm still alive.

I watched the clock as it struck six,
my broken heart I'll try to fix.

I watched the clock as it struck seven,
tell me, what's it like in heaven?

I watched the clock as it struck eight,
your garden is lovely, beyond the gate.

I watched the clock as it struck nine,
I was proud of you, that you were mine.

I watched the clock as it struck ten,
if we could have our time again.

I watched the clock as it struck eleven,
which takes me back to number seven.

I fell asleep as the clock struck twelve,
the clock is next to your picture, by my bed, upon the shelf.

David John Whitehouse

LIES

It's no good telling lies you know
You'll be found out and so remember
Always tell the truth
Or someone's temper will hit the roof
You'll get found out, so in the end
It's best to be the best of friends
And stop your lying from hence forth
It's always best to tell the truth.

Winifred Zoé Moore

WHY, OH WHY

What is the matter with people,
Why do they have to cheat and steal?
What is the matter with conscience,
Don't they care what other folks feel?

What is the matter with children,
Where are the manners we were taught?
Why are they always on the want,
Why aren't they polite as they ought?

What is wrong with our Government,
Giving money to folk who don't work?
Don't they realise that is all wrong,
It's encouraging them to shirk?

And what is wrong with our prisons,
With wrong-doers treated like kings?
Weren't they a place of detention,
For those who had all done bad things?

England was built up by hard graft,
By working from morning 'til night.
Often for just a mere pittance,
But we turned out honest and right.

Can we get back to the basics,
Of decency, honour and care?
To make us again, Great Britain,
A wonderful country to share.

Isobel Crumley

My Countryside

The sun shone down from a clear blue sky
A certain sign of spring
The birds start nesting in the trees
And as they work they sing

The farmers ploughing in the fields
Prepare to sow their crops
The days for them seem endless
As farm work never stops

The countryside looks fresh and green
From gentle showers of rain
The hedgerows full of blossom
On each side of the lane

How wonderful is nature
From seeds all good things grow
Where would we be without them
I'm sure we'll never know

Bob Reynolds

TIME AND SPACE

Though time and space may be an illusion
What a convenience the concept affords!
With our time machines synchronised we can go forward,
Space being one of its greatest rewards.

But do we assume their synchronisation?
Do we assume that it's 'All stations go'?
What of the misfits who seem out of place here?
Can their machines perhaps be fast or slow?

As we're embracing the new millennium,
All will expect to arrive dead on time,
All will assume they have come to the terminus,
Or else the beginning, when they hear the bells chime.

Olive Summerfield

THAT'S LIFE

There's a little boy called all alone
Who you'll find each night by the telephone
Still hoping that his mum will think to ring

Though he knows in his heart while she's having fun
She just won't find the time for anyone
Not even her ever loving first born son

Yet still he waits there all alone
This sad little boy by a telephone
Still hoping, that she may remember him

A J Marshall

TORMENTED SOUL

What a tormented soul
Suffering such anguish and solitude
Reaching out for understanding
For compassion
But over-estimating us
Hoping that we caring mortals
With good education
Can begin to acknowledge
The loneliness of a stricken brain
And an isolated heart.

What a tormented soul
Rolling on the waves of injustice
To live, so others may appreciate
Their own good fortune
Playing God with the ailing vessel
Patching up holes
Repairing the sails
Basking in our own versatility
While the tormented soul hungers
For a personal decision.

Sheila Sarson

THE TRAGIC TALE OF THE RED ANTS' NEST

The day my friend Mall got red ants in her pants,
She was on the phone to me,
I said, 'Whatever's the matter?'
She said, 'I don't know, I can't see.'

She kept puffing and blowing and scratching,
I said, 'Eh! now Mall, don't despair,'
She said, 'Hang on, wait a minute,'
Then she threw her pants high in the air.

Then she sighed and she said,
'Oh that's better, the blighters have bitten me leg.
And they must have bitten me ankle,
As it's swelled up just like an egg.'

For when gardening she'd sat on an ants' nest,
And they'd nested inside her pants,
It was very sad for my friend Mall,
And also quite sad for the ants.

Next she placed her pants into the washer,
I think on wash cycle one,
And then as the cycle came to an end,
Thank God, all the ants, they were gone.

So she said that the next bit of gardening,
Would be done in the broadest daylight,
So that she could see what she's doing,
And not when it's falling to night.

B G Taylor

I SEE DEATH

I'm standing on the end of the world.
Joy and pain move together.
Impermanence,
a separation from our
senses,
disenchanted, puzzled and
insecure.
Terror and fear fill me.
Everything I see is formed and
brings the danger of extinction.
Everything disappears,
beginning at birth.
This death is everywhere,
and so is beauty.
Now the birds cry
and the children call.
truth pierces matter
mind pierces spirit,
one empty moment of
insight.
This death is everywhere.

Paul Darby

POPPIES

Poppy lady once again,
Out in frost, sun and rain,
To get some money, to ease the pain,
For the soldiers who went to war.

Buy a cross or sticker for the car,
Oh! Mister how generous you are,
No, I haven't had to walk far,
For the sailors who went to war.

The tin's getting heavy, have to change hands,
Feet getting weary, but selling demands,
Not many left, just a few strands,
For the air men who went to war.

Night time is falling, weary and tired,
Nearly sold out, oh how I did try,
Rain wet poppies, hands red dyed,
For the many who went to war.

J Neville

No Answer

The unintentional rebuff
chills the heart, numbs the mind
waiting to unload despair.
Modern technology not yet designed
to sense the slow descent, unaware
of panic leering on the edge of
sanity. As if in planned collusion
Answerphones have power to dredge
the mind of reason, bring confusion
to the brink of naked tears
impossible to hide. Clutching at straws
cannot deceive a breaking heart;
search the rented line long as you may
Fate has decreed - no one's at home today.

Dorothy Thompson

SLEEPY STUFFING

On those days
when asleep and awake
are not quite separate
the dull sense of time
moves past you, somewhere
at an illegitimate rate
- where do you go?

Here in the presence
but a mind that is lost
within the tapestries of itself
like a dream of stars
a fairytale fantasy land
which remains throughout

The tiredness of heavy heads
filled with sleepy stuffing
and not even thoughts!
There's no room for thoughts today
only that drowsy, drugged
strangely calmed feeling

Too much dreaming, floating
the after-effects of deep sleep
where years could have
gone by during the night
and who would care
but the moon?

A sluggish head that won't clear
subdued idiosyncrasy
slumbering overcast
All that's left. Sleepy Stuffing.

Ali Dodds

M Is For Millennium

M is for millennium, a new life time evolves
I   is for imminent, life's lessons unfold
L   is for landmark, where we are destined to go
L   is for liberate, our freedom to show
E   is for expression, our portrayal of life
N is for nostalgia, our lives to rewrite
N is for nation, that we represent
I   is for ideology, our ideas to invent
U is for universe, there is more than ourselves
M is for memories, of what life has been
     a new century beginning of new hopes and new dreams

Jan Le Bihan Panter

HEAVEN SENT

Did an angel visit me
Or was I dreaming?
Did its breath upon my brow
Awake me, yet how
Did an angel visit me
To give life meaning?
Did I feel a hand on mine?
Were we praying?
Shafts of light were shining through
And I'm sure that it was true.
Did an angel visit me
Where I was laying?
Was I lifted from my bed
While I was sleeping?
Carried to heaven's door
To view what lay before.
An angel came to me
And I am weeping.

Josephine Burnett

READING BUDDY

A reading buddy,
I became,
The children had,
To learn my name.

They liked the stickers,
That I made,
When they read well,
To encourage I gave.

I mentioned once,
About the war,
The children looked
At me with awe.

I never thought,
To say which one,
So they believed,
It was Victorian!

So now I give,
Instructions clear,
In case they add,
Another year!

Mary McPhee

COME AWAY MA WEE GEORDIE

Come away ma wee Geordie I hear you cry
And with a smile on his face and glint in his eye
He throws back his head and giggles with glee
As I sit here and watch it's lovely to see
The effect that you have on my son so small
Whom you love as your own no question at all
You're never too busy to give him some time
When he sees you come in his little eyes shine
He knows when you get here it's time for some games
My only hope is your feelings don't change
Together you make such a natural sight
It shows on your face as his day turns to night
And he drifts off to sleep with a smile in his eyes
The love that you feel could not be disguised
Of all of the people that Jordan now knows
As a father to him you're the one that he choose.

Joanne England

THE MOON

It was early evening
A sight beyond compare
The moon enclosed
Inside a rainbow
Encircling its sphere.

The night of the moon's eclipse
That we didn't see
Clouds choking up the skies
From evening to early light
But the rainbow
About the moon
Exciting
Though only for a moment.

Mavis Smith

GET SET!

Life is short
to be wasted - *no!*

In the sparkle of youth
when you feel that glow -
'My world's an oyster'

It just ain't so!

We who have lived a
span of years
know the folly of
one's own tears,

We carry with time
our own regret -

Take heed while young -

Get set!

Mary Skelton

A BASIC NEED

Our basic need is love, we need it every day,
we would forget the bad things if I had my way.
If we shared our happiness and gave a helping hand,
the world would be a brighter place, wouldn't that be grand.
Just give a smile to show we care
and let people know that we are there.
Some of us do this, that I know,
it's a feeling that needs to grow.
Open your heart, just make a new friend,
you never know what's just round the bend.
This earth would be a better place
when each of us has a smiling face.

Alice Stapleton

A MEMORY

Two ducks on a pond
A grass bank beyond.
The blue sky of spring
White clouds on the wing.
What a little thing -
To remember for years,
To remember with tears.

Beryl Holroyd-Fidler

ALWAYS A MUM

Being a mother, what can I say,
Expectations of you differ from day to day.
Always on duty to give care at first hand,
Your life's not your own, without a plan.
The joys that motherhood can bring,
Are all forgotten when there's squabbles and din.
Your life will never be the same.
Once the patter of tiny feet enter your domain,
I'm sure the good outweighs the bad,
Just be prepared that times can be sad.
With a baby you provide all the care,
Planning life ahead, that you'll both share.
As they grow, your plans are in the past,
Your child's a little person who is growing up fast.
The years quickly pass, a teenager you see,
It seemed only yesterday that they sat on your knee.
You watch over and try to guide,
Often your advice is tossed aside.
Arguments or the silent treatment occur,
Disputes and statements 'That you don't care.'
GCSE, O and A levels gladly out of the way,
To work or uni, a decision is needed without delay.
All grown-up and leaving home,
They are still a worry, but I know I'm not alone.
Son or daughter, young or old,
A mother's love is untold.

Anne Sackey

WIRED UP

The other night I had a dream, it was a real surprise
a street was full of marching food - hams, cakes and pork pies.
A band was playing merry tunes as they went smartly past
a lamb chop held a trumpet whilst an ice-cream melted fast.
Behind a squad of sausages were sizzling in the heat
with mustard on each head and cocktail sticks for feet.
Then came a row of meaty pies, all brown and steaming hot
followed by a batch of pasties on carrot legs, running at a trot.
Next sausage rolls and pizzas all fresh and in-line
then waltzed a glass of sherry, partnered by a German wine.
There was gateaux, apple pies and trifles by the tons
chocolate eclairs, fruit slices and hordes of Chelsea buns.
Crusty loaves of fresh baked bread, with cheese and pickle feet
tasty sandwiches and filled bread rolls, all ready to eat.
Potatoes with their jackets on, others dressed as chips
Brussel sprouts and cabbages dancing with parsnips.
Tall lettuce leaves wore radishes as red polished boots
spring onions, tomatoes and round soft beetroots.
I stared in wonder at it all, yet famished as I was
not a morsel would pass my lips this night, because
my teeth were wired up in such a way, no food could pass between
my weight was swiftly dropping, I had never been this lean.
So down in heart I turned to leave this gastronomic parade
then there before me hung a sign 'Wire cutters made!'
My spirits rose, I will have food, I rushed towards the store
I was ecstatic as I walked through the door
Twas then I awoke, hot and cold, my heart filled with despair
the dream had passed, alas and the wires were still there.

Phil Aylward

MEMORIES

My memories are all about
A life so rich and full,
With laughter, tears and promises,
It was never ever dull.
I no longer get up early
But stay at home instead,
For now my time's my own
And if I wish I stay in bed.
My memory's not what it used to be,
I no longer run up stairs,
The trouble is you see
I'm old and no one cares.
Grow old gracefully they say,
Don't tint your hair with red,
Leave that touch of grey
Enhanced with silver thread.
Sometimes a friend will share my day
With a smile and a cup of tea,
I always listen to what they say
Because they're wiser than me.
Share your memories once in a while,
They are so precious and rare,
It's all you have got when you are old
And there's no one left to care.

Loraine Richmond

SOMEHOW

Somehow
She just
Walked into
His mind
That day
And there
She did
Stay
For the rest
Of his life
Having become
His wife.

W B McDade

ANCHOR BOOKS
SUBMISSIONS INVITED
SOMETHING FOR EVERYONE

ANCHOR BOOKS GEN - Any subject,
light-hearted clean fun, nothing unprintable
please.

THE OPPOSITE SEX - Have your say on the
opposite gender. Do they drive you mad or can
we co-exist in harmony?

THE NATURAL WORLD - Are we destroying
the world around us? What should we do to
preserve the beauty and the future of our planet -
you decide!

All poems no longer than 30 lines.
Always welcome! No fee!
Plus cash prizes to be won!

Mark your envelope (eg *The Natural World*)
And send to:
Anchor Books
Remus House, Coltsfoot Drive
Woodston, Peterborough, PE2 9JX

**OVER £10,000 IN POETRY PRIZES
TO BE WON!**

Send an SAE for details on our New Year 2000
competition!